SCOT HIGHTOWER

The Teen Wealth Code

Unlocking Wisdom and Prosperity

First edition

This book was professionally typeset on Reedsy.
Find out more at reedsy.com

I dedicate this book to my young grandchildren Hazel, Chris, Nick and Eva who inspired me to write this book. They have just begun their journey learning the Teen Wealth Code. I am confident it will help them unlock their financial Wisdom and Prosperity

Contents

Chapter 1: Actionable Wisdom: The Foundation of Teen Wealth

Introduction

Welcome to Chapter 1 of "The Teen Wealth Code: Unlocking Wisdom and Prosperity." In this chapter, we'll explore the fundamental principles of teen wealth and why taking action is the key to success.

Throughout our lives, we are presented with opportunities. These opportunities seldom occur at the "right time." To be successful, you must seize those opportunities by acting. Let's dive into how teens can take decisive action to unlock greater wisdom and prosperity in their lives.

Understanding Teen Wealth

Teen wealth encompasses more than just financial riches; it encompasses wisdom, personal growth, and fulfillment. In today's rapidly changing world, teenagers face numerous challenges and opportunities that shape their lives in profound ways. While financial prosperity is certainly a component of teen wealth, it is only one piece of the puzzle. It is hard to achieve financial success unless you have developed what some call a "millionaires' mindset."

Financial wealth is important because it provides teens with the resources they need to pursue their passions, support their families, and live comfortable lives. However, true wealth extends beyond monetary value and includes aspects such as emotional well-being, strong relationships, and a sense of purpose.

Emotional wealth refers to the ability to manage one's emotions effectively, build resilience in the face of adversity, and cultivate a positive mindset. Teenagers who possess emotional wealth are better equipped to navigate the ups and downs of life, form healthy relationships, and cope with stress in healthy ways.

Furthermore, personal growth is a crucial component of teen wealth. This involves continuously striving to improve oneself, develop new skills, and pursue one's passions. Teenagers who prioritize personal growth are more likely to achieve their goals, fulfill their potential, and lead fulfilling lives.

Fulfillment is perhaps the most important aspect of teen wealth. It encompasses a sense of satisfaction and contentment with one's life, derived from pursuing meaningful goals, contributing to others, and living in alignment with one's values. Teenagers who prioritize fulfillment are more likely to lead happy, fulfilling lives, regardless of their financial status.

Overall, teen wealth is about achieving a holistic sense of well-being and fulfillment in all areas of life. It involves cultivating emotional wealth, pursuing personal growth, and prioritizing fulfillment, in addition to attaining financial prosperity. By understanding and embracing the multifaceted nature of teen wealth, teenagers can lead balanced, purposeful lives that bring them joy and fulfillment.

The Importance of Action

While wisdom and prosperity are admirable goals, they remain out of reach without action. As the saying goes, "Actions speak louder than words." Teens must be willing to take bold and decisive action to turn their dreams into reality. Whether it's pursuing a passion project, starting a business, or embarking on a new adventure, action is the catalyst for transformation.

Overcoming Inertia

One of the biggest obstacles to taking action is inertia—the tendency to remain in a state of rest or inactivity. Teens often procrastinate or hesitate due to fear of failure or uncertainty about the future. However, by embracing discomfort and embracing the unknown, they can break free from inertia and move toward their goals with confidence.

The Power of Small Wins

It is important to focus on small wins to build your momentum and motivation. Teens can apply this principle by setting achievable goals and celebrating their progress along the way. Whether it's completing a challenging assignment or learning a new skill, each small win brings them closer to their vision of teen wealth.

Taking Calculated Risks

While action is essential, it's equally important for teens to take calculated risks in pursuit of their goals. This means stepping out of their comfort zones, embracing uncertainty, and learning from failure. Most people learn more from their failures than they do from their successes.

Developing a Bias Towards Action

To cultivate a mindset of action, teens must develop a bias towards action—a predisposition to take initiative and seize opportunities. This means saying yes to new experiences, seeking out challenges, and refusing to settle for mediocrity. By adopting a bias towards action, teens can unlock their full potential and create extraordinary lives.

Conclusion

In conclusion, taking action is the cornerstone of teen wealth. By understanding the importance of action, overcoming inertia, embracing small wins, taking calculated risks, and developing a bias towards action, teens can unlock greater wisdom and prosperity in their lives. By taking bold and decisive action, teens can create a life of abundance, fulfillment, and purpose.

Chapter 2: Cultivating a Millionaire Mindset for Teens

Welcome to the World of Millionaire Mindsets! In this chapter, we'll dive into the exciting journey of developing a wealthy mindset that empowers young people to achieve their dreams and create abundance in their lives. We'll explore what it means to think like a millionaire, why it's important, and how young people can cultivate this mindset to unlock their full potential.

What is a Millionaire Mindset?

A millionaire mindset is more than just about money; it's a way of thinking and approaching life that fosters success, resilience, and abundance. It involves adopting attitudes and habits that empower young people to set big goals, embrace challenges, and take action toward their dreams. With a millionaire mindset, young people learn to believe in themselves, cultivate positive thinking, and make wise choices that lead to long-term success and fulfillment.

Setting Big Goals

Dreaming Big: Encouraging young people to think boldly about their aspirations and dreams, whether it's becoming an astronaut, starting a business, or traveling the world. By dreaming big, young people expand their horizons and unlock their imaginations to envision a bright and exciting future.

Turning Dreams into Goals: Teaching young people how to turn their big dreams into actionable goals by breaking them down into smaller, achievable steps. By breaking down their goals into manageable tasks, young people can make progress toward their dreams one step at a time and stay motivated along the way.

Believing in Yourself: Building confidence in young people by helping them recognize their strengths and abilities, and instilling the belief that they have what it takes to accomplish anything they set their minds to. With a strong belief in themselves, young people can overcome obstacles and persevere in the pursuit of their goals.

Positive Thinking

The Power of Positive Thoughts: Explaining how having a positive attitude can lead to greater happiness, resilience, and success. By focusing on the bright side of life and maintaining a positive outlook, young people can overcome challenges more easily and attract opportunities that align with their goals.

Practicing Gratitude: Encouraging young people to cultivate a mindset of gratitude by focusing on the things they're thankful for each day. By practicing gratitude, young people develop a sense of appreciation for the blessings in their lives and foster a positive attitude towards themselves and others.

Seeing Challenges as Opportunities: Teaching young people to reframe challenges as opportunities for growth and learning, and to approach them with a positive mindset. By embracing challenges as stepping stones to success, young people learn to overcome adversity and emerge stronger and more resilient.

Taking Action

Putting Plans into Motion: Empowering young people to take action towards their goals by breaking them down into smaller steps and taking consistent, determined action. By taking small steps towards their dreams each day, young people make progress towards their goals and build momentum towards success.

Overcoming Fear of Failure: Helping young people understand that failure is a natural part of the learning process and encouraging them to embrace it as an opportunity to grow. By reframing failure as a valuable learning experience, young people learn to bounce back from setbacks and continue moving forward toward their goals.

Being Persistent: Teaching young people the importance of perseverance and resilience in the face of obstacles, and instilling in them the mindset of never giving up on their dreams. By staying persistent and determined, young people can overcome challenges and achieve their goals, no matter how big or daunting they may seem.

Learning and Growing

Embracing Learning Opportunities: Encouraging young people to approach every experience as an opportunity to learn and grow, and to cultivate a lifelong love of learning. By embracing learning opportunities, young people expand their knowledge, develop new skills, and unlock their potential for success.

Seeking Feedback: Teaching young people to be open to constructive feedback and to see it as a valuable tool for improvement. By seeking feedback from others, young people gain valuable insights into their strengths and areas for growth and learn how to improve and refine their skills.

Being Open-Minded: Instilling in young people the importance of being open to new ideas, perspectives, and experiences, and encouraging them to step outside of their comfort zones. By being open-minded, young people expand their horizons, broaden their perspectives, and discover new possibilities for growth and success.

Managing Money Wisely

Saving and Investing: Introducing young people to the concepts of saving money for the future and investing in assets that can grow their wealth over time. By learning to save and invest wisely, young people develop good financial habits that set them up for long-term financial success and security.

Delaying Gratification: Teaching young people the importance of patience and delayed gratification, and helping them understand that good things come to those who wait. By delaying gratification, young people learn to resist impulsive spending and prioritize long-term goals over short-term desires.

Making Smart Spending Choices: Empowering young people to make wise spending decisions by distinguishing between needs and wants, and encouraging them to prioritize their spending accordingly. By making smart spending choices, young people learn to live within their means and make their money work for them.

Surrounding Yourself with Positivity

Choosing Positive Role Models: Encouraging young people to look up to people who inspire and motivate them, and to surround themselves with positive influences. By choosing positive role models, young people learn valuable lessons and behaviors that support their growth and success.

Building Supportive Relationships: Emphasizing the importance of nurturing relationships with friends and family who believe in them and support their dreams. By surrounding themselves with supportive relationships, young people receive encouragement and guidance that helps them thrive and succeed.

Avoiding Negative Influences: Teaching young people to identify and steer clear of people or activities that bring negativity into their lives, and to focus instead on positivity and growth. By avoiding negative influences, young people protect their mindset and energy and create an environment that fosters success and abundance.

Action Items

Goal Setting: Encourage young people to write down three big goals they want to achieve and break them down into smaller, actionable steps. By setting goals, young people create a road map for success and stay focused on what they want to achieve.

Positive Affirmations: Prompt young people to start each day by expressing gratitude for three things they're thankful for and acknowledging one positive thing about themselves. By practicing positive affirmations, young people cultivate a positive mindset and build self-confidence.

Take a Risk: Challenging young people to try something new or challenging that they've been afraid to do, and to embrace the opportunity for growth and learning. By taking risks, young people step outside of their comfort zones and discover new possibilities for success.

Learn Something New: Encouraging young people to pick a topic they're interested in and learn more about it through research or by asking someone knowledgeable to teach them. By learning something new, young people expand their knowledge and develop new skills that support their growth and success.

Save Money: Empower young people to start saving money by setting up a piggy bank or savings jar and putting some money in it each week. By saving money, young people learn the value of financial responsibility and develop good money habits that set them up for future success.

Conclusion

Congratulations! You've taken the first steps towards developing a millionaire mindset that will empower you to achieve your dreams and create abundance in your life. By embracing the principles and action items outlined in this chapter, you're setting yourself up for a bright and prosperous future filled with success, happiness, and fulfillment. Remember, with the right attitude and effort, anything is possible. Keep dreaming big, believing in yourself, and taking action toward your goals, and you'll be well on your way to thinking like a millionaire!

Chapter 3: Cracking the Teen Wealth Code

Welcome to Chapter 3: Cracking the Teen Wealth Code! In this chapter, we'll delve into the essential elements of success for teens and explore how to set the stage for both financial and personal growth. By understanding these key principles, teens can unlock the secrets to building wealth and achieving their goals.

Understanding the Elements of Success

Wisdom: Wisdom is the foundation of success, encompassing knowledge, experience, and sound judgment. Teens who cultivate wisdom make informed decisions, learn from their mistakes, and navigate life's challenges with grace and resilience. By seeking out knowledge, reflecting on their experiences, and making thoughtful choices, teens can develop the wisdom they need to succeed in all areas of life.

Prosperity: Prosperity goes beyond financial wealth; it encompasses abundance in all aspects of life, including health, relationships, and personal fulfillment. Teens who strive for prosperity prioritize holistic well-being and seek to create a life that aligns with their values and passions. By cultivating gratitude, nurturing their relationships, and pursuing their dreams, teens can experience true prosperity and fulfillment in every area of their lives.

Setting the Stage for Financial and Personal Growth

Setting Clear Goals:

Action Step: Take some time to reflect on your values, passions, and aspirations. Write down three specific goals you want to achieve in the next year, five years, and ten years. Break each goal down into smaller, actionable steps.

Developing Financial Literacy:

Action Step: Educate yourself about basic financial concepts such as budgeting, saving, investing, and managing debt. Read a book or take an online course on personal finance, and commit to learning something new about money every week.

Building Healthy Habits:

Action Step: Create a daily routine that includes regular exercise, healthy eating, and good sleep hygiene. Set specific goals for each habit (e.g., exercising for 30 minutes a day, eating five servings of fruits and vegetables, getting eight hours of sleep each night), and track your progress.

Cultivating a Growth Mindset:

Action Step: Embrace challenges as opportunities for growth and learning. Whenever you encounter a setback or obstacle, ask yourself, "What can I learn from this experience?" and "How can I use this setback to become stronger and more resilient?"

Taking Action:

Action Step: Identify one small, actionable step you can take towards each of your goals. It could be opening a savings account, researching potential career paths, or starting a side hustle. Commit to taking at least one action towards your goals every day.

Practicing Gratitude:

Action Step: Start a gratitude journal and write down three things you're grateful for each day. Take a moment to reflect on the blessings in your life and express appreciation for the people, experiences, and opportunities that enrich your life.

Surrounding Yourself with Positive Influences:

Action Step: Evaluate your social circle and identify people who uplift and support you. Spend more time with positive, supportive friends and family members, and seek out mentors and role models who inspire you to pursue your dreams.

Taking Ownership of Your Future:

Action Step: Take responsibility for your actions, choices, and outcomes. Instead of blaming others or making excuses, focus on what you can control and take proactive steps towards your goals. Remember, you have the power to create the life you desire!

Conclusion

Congratulations! You've taken the first step towards cracking the teen wealth code and unlocking the secrets to success. By understanding the essential elements of success and taking action towards your goals, you're well on your way to achieving financial and personal growth. Remember to keep learning, growing, and taking proactive steps toward your dreams. With the right mindset and determination, anything is possible!

Chapter 4: Mastering Goal Setting for Teen Success

Welcome to the chapter on mastering goal setting for teen success! In this chapter, we'll explore the importance of setting goals, learn effective strategies for goal setting, and discover how teens can turn their dreams into actionable plans for success.

Understanding the Power of Goal Setting

Goal setting is the process of identifying what you want to achieve and creating a plan to make it happen. Goals give us direction, motivation, and a sense of purpose. They provide a road map for success and help us stay focused and accountable. For teens, goal setting is a powerful tool for turning dreams into reality and achieving their full potential.

Step 1: Reflect on Your Values and Passions

The first step in effective goal setting is to reflect on your values and passions. What matters most to you? What do you want to accomplish in life? Take some time to think about your dreams and aspirations, and identify the goals that align with your values and passions. Whether it's academic success, career aspirations, personal development, or relationships, setting goals that are meaningful to you will give you the motivation and drive to pursue them with passion and determination.

Step 2: Set Specific, Measurable Goals

Once you've identified your values and passions, it's time to set specific, measurable goals. A goal that is vague or undefined is difficult to achieve because there's no clear endpoint or way to measure progress. Instead, make your goals as specific and measurable as possible. For example, instead of saying "I want to get better at soccer," say "I want to improve my dribbling skills by practicing for 30 minutes every day after school." This gives you a clear target to aim for and a way to track your progress over time.

Step 3: Break Down Your Goals into Smaller Steps

Big goals can be overwhelming, but breaking them down into smaller, manageable steps makes them more achievable. Once you've set your big goals, break them down into smaller, actionable steps that you can work on every day. This not only makes your goals more manageable but also gives you a sense of progress and accomplishment as you tick off each step along the way. For example, if your goal is to get better grades, break it down into smaller steps such as studying for 30 minutes every night, completing all your homework assignments on time, and asking for help when you need it.

Step 4: Create a Plan of Action

With your goals and action steps in hand, it's time to create a plan of action. A plan outlines the specific steps you'll take to achieve your goals, including what you'll do, when you'll do it, and how you'll measure your progress. Write down your plan of action in a clear, organized format, and refer to it regularly to stay on track. Having a plan not only keeps you focused and motivated but also helps you overcome obstacles and stay accountable to yourself.

Step 5: Stay Flexible and Adapt as Needed

Finally, it's important to remember that goals are not set in stone. Life is unpredictable, and circumstances may change along the way. It's essential to stay flexible and adapt your goals and plans as needed. If you encounter obstacles or setbacks, don't get discouraged. Instead, reassess your goals, adjust your plans if necessary, and keep moving forward. Remember, setbacks are just temporary roadblocks on the journey to success, and with determination and perseverance, you can overcome them and achieve your goals.

Conclusion

Congratulations! You've learned the key steps to mastering goal setting for teen success. By reflecting on your values and passions, setting specific, measurable goals, breaking them down into smaller steps, creating a plan of action, and staying flexible and adaptable along the way, you're well on your way to achieving your dreams and living your best life. Remember, goal setting is a powerful tool for turning your dreams into reality. With determination, perseverance, and a clear plan of action, you can accomplish anything you set your mind to!

Chapter 5: Prosperity Principles: Cultivating Financial Wellness

Welcome to Chapter 5: Prosperity Principles! In this chapter, we'll explore the fundamental principles of financial prosperity and how positive financial habits can empower teens to achieve lasting wealth and well-being. By understanding the principles of financial prosperity and adopting positive financial habits, teens can lay the groundwork for a secure and prosperous future.

Introduction to Financial Prosperity

Financial prosperity goes beyond mere wealth; it encompasses the ability to live a fulfilling and abundant life. While money is certainly a part of financial prosperity, true prosperity extends to all areas of life, including health, relationships, personal growth, and community engagement. For teens, financial prosperity means having the resources and mindset to pursue their dreams, support their loved ones, and make a positive impact on the world around them.

The Power of Positive Financial Habits

Positive financial habits are the cornerstone of financial prosperity. They are the daily actions and behaviors that lead to long-term financial success and well-being. By cultivating positive financial habits early on, teens can set themselves up for a lifetime of financial security and abundance. Whether it's saving money, budgeting wisely, or investing for the future, positive financial habits are the key to unlocking financial prosperity.

Create a Budget:

Start by tracking your income and expenses for a month to get a clear picture of your spending habits. Then, create a budget that outlines how much money you'll allocate to different categories such as housing, transportation, groceries, entertainment, and savings. Be sure to set aside money for savings and emergencies, and stick to your budget as closely as possible.

Pay Yourself First:

One of the most powerful financial habits you can develop is paying yourself first. This means setting aside a portion of your income for savings and investments before paying your bills or expenses. Aim to save at least 10% of your income, 20% is better, and automate your savings if possible by setting up automatic transfers from your checking account to your savings or investment accounts.

Invest in Your Future:

Investing is a powerful way to build wealth over time. Start by educating yourself about different investment options such as stocks, bonds, mutual funds, and real estate. Consider opening a brokerage account or a retirement account such as an IRA or 401(k) and start investing regularly. Remember, the key to successful investing is to start early, diversify your investments, and stay disciplined for the long term.

Conclusion

Congratulations! You've learned the importance of financial prosperity and the power of positive financial habits. By cultivating positive financial habits such as budgeting, paying yourself first, and investing in your future, you're well on your way to achieving lasting wealth and well-being. Remember, financial prosperity is not just about money; it's about living a fulfilling and abundant life. With the right mindset and habits, you can create the life you desire and achieve your dreams.

Chapter 6: Building a Wealthy Mindset: Empowering Teens for Financial Success

Welcome to Chapter 6: Building a Wealthy Mindset! In this chapter, we'll explore how shaping teen attitudes toward money and overcoming financial fears and limiting beliefs can empower teens to cultivate a mindset of abundance and achieve financial success. By understanding the importance of mindset and adopting positive beliefs and attitudes about money, teens can overcome obstacles and unlock their full potential for wealth and prosperity.

Shaping Teen Attitudes Toward Money

Teen attitudes toward money are shaped by a variety of factors, including upbringing, culture, and personal experiences. For many teens, money can be a source of stress, anxiety, and uncertainty. However, by reframing their attitudes toward money and adopting a mindset of abundance, teens can transform their relationship with money and unlock new opportunities for financial success.

Action Steps:

Identify Your Money Mindset:

Take some time to reflect on your beliefs and attitudes toward money. Do you view money as a source of stress and worry, or as a tool for creating opportunities and achieving your goals? Write down your thoughts and feelings about money and identify any negative beliefs or attitudes that may be holding you back.

Challenge Limiting Beliefs:

Once you've identified your money mindset, challenge any limiting beliefs or negative attitudes that may be preventing you from achieving financial success. For example, if you believe that money is scarce and hard to come by, challenge yourself to shift your mindset to one of abundance and opportunity. Practice affirmations and positive self-talk to reinforce your new beliefs and attitudes about money.

Cultivate a Growth Mindset:

Adopting a growth mindset is essential for building a wealthy mindset. A growth mindset is the belief that your abilities and intelligence can be developed through effort and perseverance. Instead of viewing challenges as obstacles, see them as opportunities for growth and learning. Embrace failure as a natural part of the learning process, and use setbacks as motivation to keep pushing forward toward your goals.

Overcoming Financial Fears and Limiting Beliefs

Many teens struggle with financial fears and limiting beliefs that hold them back from achieving their full potential. Common fears include fear of failure, fear of success, fear of not having enough, and fear of making mistakes. However, by confronting these fears head-on and adopting a growth mindset, teens can overcome their limiting beliefs and unlock new opportunities for financial success.

Action Steps:

Identify Your Financial Fears:

Take some time to identify any financial fears or limiting beliefs that may be holding you back. Are you afraid of failure? Are you worried about not having enough money? Write down your fears and beliefs and acknowledge them without judgment.

Challenge Your Beliefs:

Once you've identified your financial fears and limiting beliefs, challenge them by asking yourself whether they are based on facts or assumptions. Are your beliefs about money grounded in reality, or are they based on fear and uncertainty? Challenge yourself to replace negative beliefs with positive affirmations and empowering beliefs about money and success.

Take Action Despite Your Fears:

Finally, take action despite your fears. Instead of letting fear hold you back, use it as motivation to take proactive steps toward your goals. Break your goals down into smaller, manageable steps, and take one small action every day to move closer to achieving them. Remember, courage is not the absence of fear but the willingness to act despite it.

Conclusion

Congratulations! You've learned how shaping teen attitudes toward money and overcoming financial fears and limiting beliefs can empower you to build a wealthy mindset and achieve financial success. By identifying your money mindset, challenging limiting beliefs, and taking action despite your fears, you're well on your way to unlocking new opportunities for wealth and prosperity. Remember, mindset is everything. With the right beliefs and attitudes about money, you can create the life of abundance and fulfillment you deserve.

Chapter 7: Unlocking Opportunities: Seizing Success in Every Situation

Welcome to Chapter 7: Unlocking Opportunities! In this chapter, we'll explore how to identify and seize opportunities, as well as how to turn challenges into prosperous ventures. By learning to recognize opportunities in every situation and embracing challenges as opportunities for growth and success, teens can unlock their full potential and achieve their goals.

Identifying and Seizing Opportunities

Opportunities are everywhere; the key is knowing how to recognize them and take advantage of them when they arise. Whether it's a chance to learn something new, pursue a passion, or advance in your career, opportunities can lead to growth, success, and fulfillment. By cultivating awareness and a proactive mindset, teens can learn to spot opportunities and seize them with confidence and enthusiasm.

Action Steps:

Cultivate Awareness:

The first step in identifying opportunities is to cultivate awareness of your surroundings and your interests and strengths. Pay attention to the world around you, stay curious, and be open to new experiences. Keep a journal to record your thoughts, ideas, and observations, and reflect on how you can turn them into opportunities for growth and success.

Develop a Growth Mindset:

Adopting a growth mindset is essential for recognizing and seizing opportunities. Instead of viewing challenges as obstacles, see them as opportunities for growth and learning. Embrace failure as a natural part of the learning process, and use setbacks as motivation to keep pushing forward toward your goals. Cultivate a positive attitude and a belief in your ability to overcome obstacles and achieve success.

Take Calculated Risks:

Seizing opportunities often requires taking risks, but not all risks are created equal. Instead of blindly jumping into new opportunities, take calculated risks by assessing the potential rewards and consequences. Consider the likelihood of success, the potential benefits, and the potential drawbacks before making a decision. Trust your instincts, but also rely on logic and analysis to guide your choices.

Turning Challenges into Prosperous Ventures

Challenges are inevitable in life, but they can also be opportunities for growth, innovation, and success. By reframing challenges as opportunities and approaching them with creativity and resilience, teens can turn adversity into an advantage and thrive in even the most difficult circumstances.

Action Steps:

Reframe Your Perspective:

The first step in turning challenges into prosperous ventures is to reframe your perspective. Instead of viewing challenges as problems to be avoided or overcome, see them as opportunities for growth and innovation. Shift your focus from what's wrong to what's possible, and approach challenges with a mindset of curiosity and creativity.

Embrace Failure as Feedback:

Failure is a natural part of the learning process, and it's essential for growth and success. Instead of fearing failure, embrace it as feedback and an opportunity to learn and improve. Analyze your failures objectively, identify what went wrong, and use that information to adjust your approach and make improvements. Remember, every failure brings you one step closer to success.

Seek Support and Collaboration:

Facing challenges alone can be daunting, but seeking support and collaboration can make the journey easier and more rewarding. Reach out to friends, family, mentors, and peers for guidance, advice, and encouragement. Collaborate with others who share your goals and values, and leverage their expertise, resources, and support to overcome obstacles and achieve success.

Conclusion

Congratulations! You've learned how to identify and seize opportunities, as well as how to turn challenges into prosperous ventures. By cultivating awareness, developing a growth mindset, and taking calculated risks, you can recognize opportunities and seize them with confidence and enthusiasm. Likewise, by reframing challenges as opportunities for growth and innovation, embracing failure as feedback, and seeking support and collaboration, you can turn adversity into an advantage and thrive in even the most difficult circumstances. Remember, every challenge is an opportunity in disguise. With the right mindset and approach, you can turn every situation into a stepping stone to success.

Chapter 8: Teen Entrepreneurs: Nurturing Innovation and Passion for Success

Welcome to Chapter 8: Teen Entrepreneurs! In this chapter, we'll delve into the exciting world of entrepreneurship for teens and explore how to turn passion into profit. Whether you dream of starting your own business, creating innovative products, or making a difference in your community, entrepreneurship offers endless opportunities for creativity, innovation, and success. By exploring entrepreneurship and learning how to turn your passions into profitable ventures, you can unleash your full potential and achieve your dreams.

Exploring Entrepreneurship for Teens

Entrepreneurship is more than just starting a business; it's about identifying problems, creating solutions, and making a positive impact on the world. As a teen entrepreneur, you have the unique opportunity to turn your ideas and passions into reality and create meaningful change in your community and beyond.

Whether you're interested in technology, arts, science, or social justice, entrepreneurship offers a platform for you to innovate, create, and make a difference.

Action Steps:

Identify Your Passions and Skills:

The first step in exploring entrepreneurship is to identify your passions and skills. What are you passionate about? What are you good at? Take some time to reflect on your interests, hobbies, and talents, and consider how you can turn them into opportunities for entrepreneurship. Write down your passions and skills, and brainstorm ideas for businesses or projects that align with them.

Research Entrepreneurial Opportunities:

Once you've identified your passions and skills, research entrepreneurial opportunities in your area of interest. Look for existing businesses or projects that inspire you, and study their business models, target markets, and success stories. Explore online resources, attend workshops or events, and reach out to mentors or experts in your field for guidance and advice. The more you learn about entrepreneurship, the better equipped you'll be to turn your ideas into reality.

Start Small and Experiment:

Don't be afraid to start small and experiment with different ideas and projects. Entrepreneurship is a journey of discovery and learning, and it's okay to make mistakes along the way. Start by launching a small business or project, testing your ideas in the real world, and gathering feedback from customers or users. Use this feedback to refine your ideas, iterate on your products or services, and continuously improve your entrepreneurial skills.

Turning Passion into Profit

Turning passion into profit is the ultimate goal of entrepreneurship. It's about creating value for others while pursuing your passions and interests. Whether you're selling products, providing services, or solving problems, entrepreneurship offers countless opportunities to turn your passion into profit and build a successful and fulfilling business.

Action Steps:

Identify a Problem or Need:

The first step in turning passion into profit is to identify a problem or need that you're passionate about solving. What challenges do people face in your community or industry? What solutions can you offer to address these challenges? Take some time to research and brainstorm ideas for businesses or projects that align with your passions and address real-world problems.

Create a Unique Value Proposition:

Once you've identified a problem or need, create a unique value proposition for your business or project. What sets you apart from the competition? What value do you offer to your customers or users? Develop a clear and compelling value proposition that highlights the benefits of your products or services and resonates with your target market.

Build a Strong Brand and Market Your Business:

Building a strong brand and marketing your business are essential steps in turning passion into profit. Develop a memorable brand identity that reflects your values, mission, and personality, and use it to create a consistent and cohesive brand experience across all touch points. Invest in marketing strategies that reach your target audience effectively, such as social media marketing, content marketing, and influencer partnerships. By building a strong brand and marketing your business effectively, you can attract customers, generate sales, and turn your passion into profit.

Conclusion

Congratulations! You've learned how to explore entrepreneurship for teens and turn passion into profit. By identifying your passions and skills, researching entrepreneurial opportunities, starting small, and experimenting with different ideas, you can embark on your entrepreneurial journey with confidence and enthusiasm. Likewise, by identifying a problem or need, creating a unique value proposition, building a strong brand, and marketing your business effectively, you can turn your passion into profit and build a successful and fulfilling business. Remember, entrepreneurship is about more than just making money; it's about making a difference and creating a legacy that lasts. With dedication, creativity, and perseverance, you can achieve your entrepreneurial dreams and make a positive impact on the world.

Chapter 9: Financial Literacy for Teens: Empowering Financial Independence

Welcome to Chapter 9: Financial Literacy for Teens! In this chapter, we'll dive into the essential money management skills and basic financial concepts that every teen should know to achieve financial independence and success. By mastering these foundational principles of financial literacy, teens can take control of their finances, make informed decisions, and build a secure and prosperous future. Remember, as long as you spend less money than you earn, you'll always have enough money!

Money Management Skills

Money management skills are the foundation of financial literacy. They encompass the ability to budget, save, spend wisely, and plan for the future. By developing these essential skills, teens can effectively manage their finances and achieve their financial goals.

Action Steps:

Create a Budget:

The first step in mastering money management is to create a budget. Start by tracking your income and expenses for a month to get a clear picture of your spending habits. Then, create a budget that outlines how much money you'll allocate to different categories such as housing, transportation, groceries, entertainment, and savings. Be sure to set aside money for savings and emergencies and stick to your budget as closely as possible.

Three common budgeting methods are:

The 50/30/20 Rule:

This budgeting method allocates your income into three main categories: needs, wants, and savings/debt repayment.

- 50% of your income goes toward needs, which are essential expenses such as rent/mortgage, utilities, groceries, transportation, and insurance.
- 30% of your income is allocated to wants, which are non-essential expenses such as dining out, entertainment, shopping, and vacations.
- The remaining 20% of your income is dedicated to savings and debt repayment, including contributions to savings

accounts, retirement funds, and paying off debt.

Example: If your monthly income is $3000, you would allocate $1500 (50%) to needs, $900 (30%) to wants, and $600 (20%) to savings or debt repayment.

Zero-Based Budgeting:

In zero-based budgeting, every dollar of income is allocated to specific categories, leaving no money unassigned.

- You start with your total income for the month and assign every dollar to expenses, savings, or debt repayment until you reach zero.
- This method requires careful tracking and planning, as you need to ensure that your expenses match your income exactly.
- Zero-based budgeting encourages you to prioritize your spending based on your financial goals and values.

Example: If your monthly income is $4000, you would allocate all $4000 to various categories such as rent, groceries, utilities, transportation, savings, and debt repayment until you have accounted for every dollar.

Envelope Budgeting:

Envelope budgeting involves dividing your cash into physical envelopes labeled with different spending categories.

- Each envelope represents a specific expense category, such as groceries, transportation, dining out, entertainment, and savings.
- You allocate a certain amount of cash to each envelope based on your budget for that category.
- Once an envelope is empty, you cannot spend any more money in that category until the next budgeting period.
- Envelope budgeting helps you visually track your spending and prevents overspending in certain categories.

Example: If your budget for groceries is $300 per month, you would put $300 in cash into the "groceries" envelope. Once you have spent all the cash in that envelope, you cannot buy any more groceries until the next month or until you reallocate funds from another envelope.

Save Money:

Saving money is an essential money management skill that every teen should master. Aim to save at least 10% of your income, and automate your savings if possible by setting up automatic transfers from your checking account to your savings or investment accounts. Start by setting short-term savings goals, such as saving for a new gadget or a fun experience, and then gradually work your way up to longer-term goals, such as saving for college or a car.

Practice Smart Spending:

Spending money wisely is another key money management skill. Before making a purchase, ask yourself if it's something you really need or just something you want. Consider the value that the purchase will bring to your life, and weigh it against the cost. Look for ways to save money, such as shopping around for the best deals, using coupons or discount codes, and avoiding impulse purchases. By practicing smart spending, you can make the most of your money and stretch your dollars further.

Understanding Basic Financial Concepts

Understanding basic financial concepts is crucial for making informed financial decisions and navigating the complexities of the modern financial world. From budgeting and saving to investing and credit, teens need to have a solid grasp of these concepts to build a strong foundation for financial success.

Action Steps:

Learn About Budgeting:

Budgeting is the process of planning and managing your finances to achieve your financial goals. Learn about the key components of a budget, such as income, expenses, savings, and discretionary spending. Explore different budgeting methods, such as the 50/30/20 rule or zero-based budgeting, and find a method that works best for you. Practice creating and managing a budget, and track your progress over time to see how your financial situation improves.

Explore Saving and Investing:

Saving and investing are essential components of financial planning. Learn about the importance of saving money for emergencies, short-term goals, and long-term goals such as retirement. Explore different savings vehicles, such as savings accounts, certificates of deposit (CDs), and individual retirement accounts (IRAs), and choose the ones that best suit your needs and goals. Similarly, learn about the basics of investing, such as stocks, bonds, mutual funds, and real estate, and explore different investment strategies to grow your wealth over time.

Understand Credit and Debt:

Credit and debt are important financial concepts that can have a significant impact on your financial health. Learn about the basics of credit, such as credit scores, credit reports, and credit cards, and understand how to use credit responsibly to build a positive credit history. Similarly, learn about the basics of debt, such as loans, mortgages, and interest rates, and understand the importance of managing debt wisely to avoid financial pitfalls. By understanding credit and debt, you can make informed decisions about borrowing and lending money and avoid falling into debt traps.

Conclusion

Congratulations! You've learned the essential money management skills and basic financial concepts that every teen should know to achieve financial independence and success. By mastering these foundational principles of financial literacy, you can take control of your finances, make informed decisions, and build a secure and prosperous future. Remember, financial literacy is the key to unlocking financial freedom and achieving your dreams. With dedication, discipline, and determination, you can build a strong foundation for financial success and achieve your goals.

Chapter 10: Investing in Your Future: Building Long-Term Prosperity

Welcome to Chapter 10: Investing in Your Future! In this chapter, we'll explore the world of investing and how teens can start building long-term prosperity for themselves. By understanding the basics of investing and creating a plan for their financial future, teens can set themselves up for success and achieve their long-term goals.

Introduction to Teen-Friendly Investments

Investing is the process of putting money into assets with the expectation of generating returns over time. While investing may seem intimidating at first, there are many teen-friendly investment options available that can help teens grow their wealth and achieve their financial goals.

Action Steps:

Understand the Basics of Investing:

Start by learning the basics of investing, including different types of investments such as stocks, bonds, mutual funds, and real estate. Understand the concept of risk and return, and how it applies to investing. Learn about the importance of diversification and how to build a well-balanced investment portfolio.

Explore Teen-Friendly Investment Options:

There are many investment options available that are suitable for teens, including custodial accounts, brokerage accounts, and retirement accounts such as Roth IRAs. Research different investment platforms and providers, and choose one that offers low fees, a user-friendly interface, and a wide range of investment options.

Start Small and Invest Consistently:

Start small by investing a portion of your savings into teen-friendly investments. Consider starting with low-risk investments such as index funds or exchange-traded funds (ETFs), which offer diversification and stability. Set up automatic contributions to your investment account and invest consistently over time. Remember, the key to successful investing is to start early and invest regularly.

Planning for Long-Term Prosperity

Planning for long-term prosperity involves setting financial goals, creating a plan to achieve them, and making smart investment decisions that align with your goals and risk tolerance. By taking a proactive approach to investing and planning for the future, teens can build wealth and achieve financial independence over time.

Action Steps:

Set Long-Term Financial Goals:

Start by setting long-term financial goals that reflect your aspirations and values. Whether it's saving for college, buying a home, starting a business, or retiring early, having clear goals will help you stay focused and motivated. Break down your goals into smaller, actionable steps, and create a timeline for achieving them.

Create a Financial Plan:

Once you've set your financial goals, create a comprehensive financial plan that outlines how you will achieve them. Determine how much money you need to save and invest each month to reach your goals, and identify the best investment strategies and vehicles to help you get there. Consider working with a financial advisor or planner to create a personalized plan that aligns with your goals and risk tolerance.

Monitor and Adjust Your Plan Regularly:

Finally, monitor your progress regularly and make adjustments to your plan as needed. Review your investment portfolio periodically to ensure it remains aligned with your goals and risk tolerance. If your circumstances or goals change, update your financial plan accordingly. By staying proactive and flexible, you can adapt to changing circumstances and stay on track to achieve your long-term financial goals.

Conclusion

Congratulations! You've learned how to invest in your future and build long-term prosperity for yourself. By understanding the basics of investing, exploring teen-friendly investment options, and starting small and investing consistently, you can lay the foundation for a secure and prosperous future. Likewise, by setting long-term financial goals, creating a comprehensive financial plan, and monitoring and adjusting your plan regularly, you can stay on track to achieve your goals and build wealth over time. Remember, investing is a journey, not a destination. With patience, discipline, and dedication, you can achieve financial independence and create the life of your dreams.

Chapter 11: Navigating Teen Expenses: Mastering Budgeting and Smart Spending

Welcome to Chapter 11: Navigating Teen Expenses! In this chapter, we'll explore the essential skills of budgeting for teenagers and making smart spending choices. By mastering these skills, teens can effectively manage their expenses, make informed financial decisions, and achieve their financial goals.

Budgeting for Teenagers

Budgeting is the cornerstone of financial management and involves tracking income and expenses to ensure that spending aligns with financial goals. For teenagers, budgeting provides a valuable opportunity to learn money management skills and develop responsible financial habits.

Action Steps:

Track Your Income and Expenses:

Start by tracking your income and expenses to get a clear understanding of your financial situation. Keep track of all sources of income, such as allowances, part-time jobs, or gifts, as well as all expenses, including necessities like food, transportation, and school supplies, as well as discretionary spending on entertainment, clothes, and hobbies.

Create a Budget:

Once you've tracked your income and expenses, create a budget that outlines how you will allocate your money. Start by categorizing your expenses into needs (essential expenses) and wants (discretionary expenses), and allocate a portion of your income to each category. Be sure to set aside money for savings and emergencies, and prioritize your spending based on your financial goals and priorities.

Stick to Your Budget:

Once you've created a budget, stick to it as closely as possible. Track your spending regularly to ensure that you're staying within your budgeted amounts for each category. If you find yourself overspending in certain areas, look for ways to cut back or reallocate funds to stay on track. Remember, budgeting is a tool to help you achieve your financial goals, so make adjustments as needed to ensure that your budget reflects your priorities and values.

Making Smart Spending Choices

Making smart spending choices involves evaluating purchases based on their value and importance and prioritizing spending to align with financial goals and priorities. By practicing smart spending, teens can make the most of their money and achieve their financial goals more quickly and efficiently.

Action Steps:

Differentiate Between Needs and Wants:

One of the key principles of smart spending is differentiating between needs (essential expenses) and wants (discretionary expenses). Before making a purchase, ask yourself if it's something you truly need or just something you want. Consider the value that the purchase will bring to your life and prioritize spending on needs over wants.

Comparison Shop and Look for Deals:

When making purchases, take the time to comparison shop and look for the best deals. Compare prices from different retailers, both online and in-store, and look for discounts, sales, and promotions. Consider using coupons, promo codes, or cashback offers to save money on purchases. By being savvy and resourceful, you can stretch your dollars further and get more value for your money.

Practice Delayed Gratification:

Delayed gratification is the practice of postponing immediate rewards or pleasures in favor of long-term goals or benefits. Instead of giving in to impulse purchases or instant gratification, take the time to think about whether the purchase aligns with your financial goals and priorities. If it's not a necessity, consider delaying the purchase and saving up for it instead. By practicing delayed gratification, you can avoid overspending and make more thoughtful and intentional spending decisions.

Conclusion

Congratulations! You've learned how to navigate teen expenses by mastering budgeting and making smart spending choices. By tracking your income and expenses, creating a budget, and sticking to it, you can effectively manage your finances and achieve your financial goals. Likewise, by differentiating between needs and wants, comparison shopping, and practicing delayed gratification, you can make the most of your money and get closer to your financial goals. Remember, smart spending is about making intentional choices that align with your values and priorities, so take the time to evaluate your spending decisions and make adjustments as needed. With practice and discipline, you can become a savvy and responsible spender and achieve financial success.

Chapter 12: The Path to Teen Success: Achieving Goals and Cultivating Balance

Welcome to Chapter 12: The Path to Teen Success! In this chapter, we'll explore the essential elements of achieving success as a teenager, including setting and achieving goals and cultivating a balanced life. By mastering these skills, teens can unlock their full potential, pursue their passions, and create a fulfilling and meaningful life.

Setting and Achieving Goals

Setting and achieving goals is a fundamental skill that can propel teens toward success and fulfillment. By setting clear and actionable goals, teens can focus their efforts, stay motivated, and track their progress toward their aspirations.

Action Steps:

Define Your Goals:

Start by defining your goals based on your passions, interests, and values. Think about what you want to achieve in different areas of your life, such as academics, extracurricular activities, relationships, and personal development. Write down your goals and make them specific, measurable, achievable, relevant, and time-bound (SMART).

Create an Action Plan:

Once you've defined your goals, create an action plan outlining the steps you need to take to achieve them. Break down your goals into smaller, actionable tasks, and set deadlines for each task. Identify any obstacles or challenges you may face along the way and develop strategies to overcome them. By having a clear plan of action, you can stay organized and focused on reaching your goals.

Take Consistent Action:

The key to achieving goals is taking consistent action towards them. Commit to taking small, incremental steps each day towards your goals, even when you don't feel motivated or inspired. Stay disciplined and focused on your priorities, and celebrate your progress along the way. Remember, every step you take brings you closer to your dreams.

Cultivating a Balanced Life

Cultivating a balanced life involves finding harmony and fulfillment in all areas of your life, including academics, extracurricular activities, relationships, and personal well-being. By prioritizing self-care, time management, and work-life balance, teens can thrive academically, socially, and emotionally.

Action Steps:

Prioritize Self-Care:

Make self-care a priority by taking care of your physical, mental, and emotional well-being. Get enough sleep, eat nutritious foods, exercise regularly, and practice relaxation techniques such as meditation or deep breathing. Make time for activities that bring you joy and relaxation, such as hobbies, spending time with loved ones, or enjoying nature.

Manage Your Time Wisely:

Time management is essential for maintaining a balanced life. Prioritize your tasks and responsibilities based on their importance and deadlines, and create a schedule or to-do list to help you stay organized and focused. Use time-blocking techniques to allocate specific blocks of time for different activities, and avoid procrastination by breaking tasks into smaller, manageable chunks.

Foster Meaningful Relationships:

Building and maintaining meaningful relationships is crucial for a balanced life. Invest time and effort in nurturing your relationships with family, friends, teachers, and mentors. Be present and engaged in your interactions, listen actively, and offer support and encouragement to others. Surround yourself with positive and supportive people who uplift and inspire you.

Conclusion

Congratulations! You've learned how to navigate the path to teen success by setting and achieving goals and cultivating a balanced life. By defining your goals, creating an action plan, and taking consistent action toward your aspirations, you can turn your dreams into reality and achieve success in all areas of your life. Likewise, by prioritizing self-care, managing your time wisely, and fostering meaningful relationships, you can create a balanced and fulfilling life that brings you joy and fulfillment. Remember, success is not just about achieving external milestones but also about finding happiness, fulfillment, and purpose in everything you do. With dedication, discipline, and determination, you can chart your path to success and create a life that reflects your true potential and aspirations.

Chapter 13: The Path to Teen Success: Secure Your Financial Freedom First!

Welcome to Chapter 13: Secure Your Financial Freedom First! In this chapter, we will delve into the fundamental principles of financial freedom and explore actionable strategies for achieving it. By understanding the concepts of financial freedom, implementing the "pay yourself first" principle, and overcoming common challenges on the path to financial independence, teens can build a solid foundation for long-term wealth and prosperity.

Understanding Financial Freedom

Financial freedom is the ultimate goal of financial planning. It is the state of being where an individual has enough passive income to cover all living expenses without needing to work actively for a paycheck. Achieving financial freedom provides individuals with the freedom to pursue their passions, spend time with loved ones, and live life on their own terms.

Definition of Financial Freedom:

Financial freedom is the ability to maintain a desired lifestyle without being dependent on employment income. It means having enough wealth and passive income streams to cover all living expenses, allowing individuals to pursue their interests and goals without financial constraints.

Importance of Financial Independence:

Financial independence is a crucial component of financial freedom. It is the ability to support oneself and one's lifestyle without relying on external sources of income. Financial independence provides individuals with security, autonomy, and the freedom to make choices based on their priorities and values.

The Pay Yourself First Principle in Action

The "pay yourself first" principle is a foundational strategy for achieving financial freedom. It involves prioritizing savings and investments by allocating a portion of income before paying for any other expenses. By paying yourself first, you ensure that you are building wealth and securing your financial future.

How Paying Yourself First Contributes to Financial Freedom:

Paying yourself first is a proactive approach to wealth-building. By prioritizing savings and investments, individuals can gradually accumulate wealth over time and create a financial safety net for themselves. Paying yourself first also instills discipline and ensures that saving becomes a habit rather than an afterthought.

Real-Life Examples of Individuals Achieving Financial Independence:

Many individuals have achieved financial independence by following the pay-yourself-first principle. From early retirement enthusiasts to successful entrepreneurs, these individuals have demonstrated that financial freedom is attainable with discipline, patience, and strategic financial planning.

Strategies for Securing Financial Freedom

Building emergency savings and investing in income-generating assets are essential strategies for securing financial freedom. Emergency savings provide a financial safety net in case of unexpected expenses or loss of income, while income-generating assets generate passive income that can cover living expenses.

Building Emergency Savings:

Start by setting aside a portion of your income into a dedicated emergency savings account. Aim to save enough to cover three to six months' worth of living expenses. Treat emergency savings as a non-negotiable expense and prioritize building this fund before allocating funds to other financial goals.

Investing in Income-Generating Assets:

Invest in assets that have the potential to generate passive income, such as stocks, bonds, real estate, or business ventures. Diversify investments to spread risk and maximize returns. Regularly review and adjust investment strategies to align with changing financial goals and market conditions.

Overcoming Challenges on the Path to Financial Freedom

Dealing with debt and managing lifestyle inflation are common challenges on the path to financial freedom. By addressing these challenges and adopting prudent financial habits, individuals can overcome obstacles and stay on track toward achieving their financial goals.

Dealing with Debt:

Develop a plan to pay off outstanding debts, starting with high-interest debt. Consider strategies such as debt consolidation or refinancing to lower interest rates and make payments more manageable. Avoid taking on new debt and focus on reducing existing debt to accelerate progress towards financial freedom.

Managing Lifestyle Inflation:

Lifestyle inflation occurs when spending increases as income rises, leading to a higher cost of living and reduced savings rate. To combat lifestyle inflation, practice living below your means and avoid unnecessary expenses. Prioritize saving and investing to ensure that increased income leads to greater financial security and wealth accumulation.

Action Steps:

Calculate Your Financial Independence Number:

Determine the amount of wealth needed to achieve financial independence by calculating your financial independence number. Consider factors such as living expenses, desired lifestyle, and expected investment returns to determine the target savings and investment goals required for financial freedom.

Develop a Plan to Achieve Financial Freedom, Starting with Paying Yourself First:

Create a comprehensive financial plan outlining steps to achieve financial freedom. Start by paying yourself first and automating savings and investments to ensure consistency. Set specific savings and investment targets and track progress regularly. Adjust the plan as needed to stay on track toward achieving financial independence.

Review and Adjust Financial Plan Regularly:

Regularly review and adjust financial plans to reflect changes in goals, priorities, and financial circumstances. Monitor savings and investment progress, and make adjustments as needed to stay on track toward achieving financial freedom. Seek guidance from financial advisors or mentors to ensure that plans are aligned with long-term financial goals.

Conclusion

Congratulations! You have completed Chapter 13: Secure Your Financial Freedom First. By understanding the principles of financial freedom, implementing the "pay yourself first" principle, and adopting actionable strategies for achieving financial independence, you have laid a solid foundation for long-term wealth and prosperity. Remember, financial freedom is within reach for anyone willing to commit to disciplined saving, strategic investing, and prudent financial planning. With dedication, perseverance, and a clear vision for the future, you can achieve financial independence and create the life of your dreams.

Chapter 14: The Magic of Compound Interest: Building Wealth Through Time

Welcome to Chapter 14: The Magic of Compound Interest! In this chapter, we will uncover the incredible power of compound interest and explore how it can be leveraged to build wealth over time. As Albert Einstein famously said, "Compound interest is the eighth wonder of the world." Let's dive deep into understanding this concept and discover how it can work in your favor.

Understanding the Power of Compound Interest

Explanation of Compound Interest:

Compound interest is the process where interest is earned not only on the initial principal investment but also on the accumulated interest from previous periods. In simpler terms, it's interest on interest, which allows your money to grow exponentially over time. The longer your money is invested, the more significant the impact of compound interest becomes.

Examples of Compound Interest in Action:

Let's consider an example to illustrate the power of compound interest. Suppose you invest $1,000 in an account that earns an annual interest rate of 5%. At the end of the first year, you would earn $50 in interest, bringing your total balance to $1,050. In the second year, you earn 5% interest not just on the initial $1,000 but also on the $50 of interest earned in the first year. This compounding effect continues to grow your wealth over time.

Einstein's Perspective: "Compound Interest is the Eighth Wonder of the World."

Explanation of Einstein's Quote:

Albert Einstein famously referred to compound interest as the eighth wonder of the world because of its remarkable ability to multiply wealth over time. The concept fascinated him because it demonstrated the power of mathematics to generate wealth passively. Einstein recognized that those who understand and harness the power of compound interest could achieve financial abundance beyond imagination.

Illustrative Story or Anecdote:

Consider the story of two friends, Alex and Ben. Alex starts investing $100 per month at age 25 and continues until he's 35, stopping after ten years. Ben, on the other hand, procrastinates and doesn't start investing until age 35. He invests the same $100 per month but continues until he's 65, investing for thirty years. Despite investing for half the time, Alex ends up with significantly more wealth at retirement age due to the magic of compound interest.

Action Steps:

Use a compound interest calculator to see the impact of regular savings over time:

Take advantage of online compound interest calculators to visualize how your savings can grow over time. Input your initial investment, monthly contributions, interest rate, and investment horizon to see the projected growth of your wealth. This exercise will highlight the importance of consistent saving and the power of compounding.

Set a long-term savings goal and calculate how much you need to save each month to achieve it:

Determine your financial goals, whether it's saving for retirement, purchasing a home, or funding your education. Use compound interest calculations to reverse engineer your savings plan. Calculate how much you need to save each month to reach your target amount by a specific deadline. Breaking down your goals into manageable monthly contributions makes them more achievable.

Start investing early and regularly:

The most crucial action step is to start investing as early as possible and make regular contributions. Time is your most valuable asset when it comes to compound interest. Even small contributions made consistently over time can grow into substantial wealth. Take advantage of retirement accounts, such as 401(k)s or IRAs, and set up automatic contributions to ensure consistent investing.

Conclusion

Congratulations! You've completed Chapter 14: The Magic of Compound Interest. By understanding the concept of compound interest and its exponential growth potential, you've gained a powerful tool for building wealth over time. As Albert Einstein recognized, compound interest is truly the eighth wonder of the world, capable of transforming modest savings into substantial wealth with patience and consistency. Remember, the key to harnessing the power of compound interest is to start early, invest regularly, and let time work its magic. With dedication and a long-term perspective, you can achieve your financial goals and create a secure and prosperous future for yourself.

Chapter 15: Mastering Negotiation: A Guide for Young people

Welcome to Chapter 15: Mastering Negotiation! In this chapter, we will delve into the world of negotiation and equip you with the skills and tactics needed to become a confident and effective negotiator. Negotiation is an essential life skill that can help you achieve your goals, resolve conflicts, and build stronger relationships. Let's face it, as a teen, almost everything you need or want is controlled by others, family, school, friends, etc. To get what you want, you must negotiate for what you want, whether it's a later curfew, permission to skip a class, or a ride to a party. Let's dive in and discover the art of negotiation!

Understanding Needs and Wants

Explaining Needs vs. Wants:

Needs are essential for survival, such as food, shelter, and clothing, while wants are things that we desire but are not necessary for survival, like toys or gadgets. Understanding the difference between needs and wants is crucial for effective negotiation.

For example, if negotiating for a new toy, acknowledge that it's a want, not a need, and be prepared to prioritize accordingly.

Identifying Your Own Needs and Wants:

Take some time to reflect on your own needs and wants before entering into a negotiation. What are your priorities and goals? Knowing what you want to achieve will help you negotiate more effectively. If negotiating for a later bedtime, identify why it's important to you, such as having more time to finish homework or read before sleep.

Recognizing the Needs and Wants of Others:

In addition to understanding your own needs and wants, it's essential to empathize with the other party's perspective. Consider their interests and priorities to find mutually beneficial solutions during negotiations. For instance, if negotiating chores with a sibling, acknowledge their desire for fairness and balance in workload.

Preparation is Key

Setting Your Goals for the Negotiation:

Before entering into a negotiation, clearly define your objectives and what you hope to achieve. Setting specific goals will help you stay focused and guide your negotiation strategy. For example, if negotiating for more screen time, determine how much additional time you're aiming for and what activities you'll use it for.

Gathering Information:

Research the topic or issue you'll be negotiating about to gather relevant information and data. The more informed you are, the better equipped you'll be to make persuasive arguments and negotiate effectively. If negotiating for a later bedtime, gather information about the benefits of sufficient sleep for your health and academic performance.

Role-playing Negotiations with a Friend or Family Member:

Practice negotiating with a friend or family member through role-playing scenarios. This exercise will help you become more comfortable with the negotiation process and refine your communication and problem-solving skills. Practice negotiating scenarios like sharing toys or deciding on a family movie night to improve your negotiation skills.

Building Rapport

Listening to the Other Person:

Actively listen to the other party's concerns and perspectives during the negotiation. Pay attention to what they say and demonstrate that you value their input by listening attentively. For instance, if negotiating a compromise with a friend, listen to their reasons for their position and acknowledge their perspective.

Finding Common Ground:

Look for areas of agreement or shared interests that can serve as a foundation for negotiation. Finding common ground helps build rapport and fosters a collaborative atmosphere during negotiations. If negotiating with a classmate about a group project, find shared goals or interests in the project's outcome to build rapport.

Being Polite and Respectful:

Maintain a polite and respectful demeanor throughout the negotiation process. Use please and thank you when making requests, and avoid interrupting or speaking over the other party. A respectful attitude goes a long way in building trust and goodwill. If negotiating with a teacher for extra credit, maintain a respectful tone and express gratitude for their consideration.

75

Using Effective Communication

Expressing Yourself Clearly:

Communicate your thoughts and ideas clearly and concisely using simple language and gestures that are easy to understand. Avoid using jargon or complex terminology that may confuse the other party. For example, if negotiating for a later curfew, clearly articulate your reasons, such as increased responsibility and trustworthiness.

Asking Questions:

Ask open-ended questions to gain a deeper understanding of the other party's perspective and interests. Listen actively to their responses and use probing questions to clarify any points of confusion. If negotiating with a parent for more allowance, ask questions to understand their concerns and explore potential compromises.

Using Positive Body Language:

Use positive body language, such as smiling, making eye contact, and maintaining an open posture, to convey confidence and warmth during negotiations. Positive body language can help build rapport and establish a positive atmosphere for negotiation. Maintain positive body language throughout the negotiation process to convey confidence and sincerity.

Creative Problem Solving

Brainstorming Solutions Together:

Collaborate with the other party to generate creative solutions to the problem at hand. Encourage brainstorming and consider all ideas, no matter how unconventional they may seem. If negotiating with a friend about which game to play, brainstorm different options and discuss the pros and cons of each.

Compromising:

Be willing to compromise and find a middle ground that satisfies both parties' interests. Consider what concessions you're willing to make and prioritize achieving a mutually beneficial outcome. If negotiating with a sibling about sharing a bedroom, be open to compromises such as alternating nights or sharing common areas.

Being Flexible and Open-minded:

Remain flexible and open-minded throughout the negotiation process. Be willing to adapt your approach and consider alternative solutions that may better meet both parties' needs. If negotiating with a teacher about a deadline extension, be open to alternative solutions such as completing extra credit assignments or adjusting the project requirements.

Making Win-Win Solutions

Finding Solutions that Benefit Both Parties:

Aim to create win-win solutions that satisfy the interests of both parties involved. Look for creative ways to maximize value and create mutual gains during negotiations. If negotiating with a friend about sharing a toy, explore options that allow both parties to enjoy the toy at different times or share ownership.

Celebrating Agreements Reached:

Celebrate successful negotiations and agreements reached with the other party. Acknowledge the effort and cooperation that went into finding a resolution and express gratitude for their collaboration. If negotiating a compromise with a classmate, celebrate reaching a mutual agreement and express appreciation for their willingness to collaborate.

Understanding that Compromise is Okay:

Recognize that compromise is a natural part of the negotiation process. Be willing to make concessions and find compromises that allow both parties to achieve their most important objectives. If negotiating with a parent about household chores, be open to compromise and find solutions that balance responsibilities and preferences.

Dealing with Disagreements

Staying Calm and Patient:

Maintain a calm and patient demeanor, even in the face of disagreement or conflict. Take deep breaths and remain composed to avoid escalating tensions during negotiations. If disagreements arise during negotiation, take a moment to pause and regain composure before addressing them calmly and rationally.

Listening to the Other Person's Perspective:

Actively listen to the other person's perspective, even if you disagree with their position. Seek to understand their concerns and motivations to find common ground and resolve disagreements constructively. If disagreements arise during negotiation, actively listen to the other party's perspective and demonstrate empathy and understanding.

The following are 20 of the top negotiating tactics you can use. Use one of them or combine them to finalize the deal!

Anchoring: This tactic involves setting an initial offer or "anchor" that influences subsequent negotiations. For example, if you're selling a used video game console, you might start with a higher price than you expect to receive, allowing room for negotiation down to your desired price.

Mirroring: Mirroring involves subtly reflecting the body language, tone, or language of the person you're negotiating with to build rapport and establish a connection. For instance, if the other party leans forward and speaks enthusiastically, you might mirror their posture and energy level to create a sense of alignment.

Flattery: Complimenting the other party or expressing admiration for their skills or accomplishments can help create a positive atmosphere and foster goodwill during negotiations. For example, you might compliment a colleague on their innovative ideas before discussing a project collaboration.

Silence: Silence can be a powerful negotiation tactic, as it encourages the other party to fill the void with concessions or additional information. Practice comfortable silence after making an offer or counteroffer to give the other party space to respond.

Nodding: Nodding subtly during negotiations can convey agreement or encouragement, influencing the other party's perception of your position. Use strategic nods to signal approval or understanding during key points in the negotiation process.

Framing: Framing involves presenting information or framing the discussion in a way that favors your position and influences the other party's perception. For example, framing a salary negotiation in terms of industry standards or cost-of-living increases can support your desired salary range.

Limited Authority: Claiming limited authority to make decisions or concessions during negotiations can give you flexibility and room to maneuver. For instance, you might say, "I'll need to check with my manager before I can agree to that," allowing you to consult with others before finalizing terms.

Bundling: Bundling involves combining multiple items or concessions into a package deal to create perceived value and encourage agreement. For example, offering a discount on a product bundle can incentivize the other party to agree to the entire package rather than individual items.

Walk Away: Demonstrating a willingness to walk away from the negotiation table can convey confidence and signal that you have alternatives or are not desperate for a deal. However, use this tactic judiciously and be prepared to follow through if necessary.

Time Pressure: Creating artificial time pressure or deadlines can motivate the other party to make concessions or agree to terms more quickly. For instance, you might mention that you have other offers on the table or that prices will increase after a certain date to encourage prompt decision-making.

Bracketing: Bracketing involves proposing extreme or ambitious initial offers with the expectation of meeting somewhere in the middle. This tactic allows both parties to make concessions while still feeling like they've achieved a favorable outcome. The other party often offers to split the difference between the two offers. Combine with the silence strategy to let the other party negotiate against themselves. Wait for it.

But if they don't say anything, point out the "new range" with your offer and their revised one. Then say we are so close. They may offer to split the difference again. Repeat the offer out loud. Say "Well that's better" and continue to negotiate. Perhaps raise your offer a little, less than ½ the difference, and see what happens.

This is not Good: works in service industries when something is wrong. I used this tactic when my food came out after almost everyone in my family had eaten most of theirs. I used this phrase and the manager came over and comped several desserts for the table to share. A win-win solution!

Take It or Leave It: Presenting a non-negotiable offer or ultimatum can be an effective tactic when you have a strong position or limited flexibility. However, use this tactic cautiously, as it can damage relationships and lead to an impasse if not handled delicately.

Leverage: Identify and leverage sources of power or advantage to strengthen your position in negotiations. This could include factors such as scarcity of resources, expertise, or competitive offers from other parties.

Questioning: Asking strategic questions can elicit valuable information, uncover hidden interests, and guide the direction of negotiations. Use open-ended questions to encourage the other party to share their perspective and concerns.

Nibbling: Nibbling involves making small, last-minute requests or concessions after the main terms of the agreement have been settled. For example, you might ask for complimentary upgrades or additional services as a final touch to sweeten the deal.

Good Cop, Bad Cop: Involving multiple negotiators with contrasting roles can create dynamic tension and influence the other party's perceptions. One negotiator can play the "good cop," while the other takes a more assertive or challenging stance.

Escalation of Commitment: Encouraging the other party to invest time, effort, or resources into the negotiation process can create a sense of commitment and increase their willingness to reach an agreement. For example, suggesting collaborative brainstorming sessions or sharing detailed proposals can deepen engagement and commitment.

Conditional Offers: Making conditional offers that are contingent on specific conditions or requirements being met can protect your interests and mitigate risks during negotiations. For instance, you might offer a discount on bulk purchases if the other party agrees to a long-term contract.

Walk in Their Shoes: Empathizing with the other party's perspective and demonstrating an understanding of their needs and interests can build trust and facilitate collaboration. Take time to consider the negotiation from their point of view and address their concerns respectfully.

Post-settlement Settlements: After reaching a preliminary agreement, revisit the terms and propose additional concessions or adjustments to further optimize the deal. This tactic allows both parties to fine-tune the agreement and address any remaining concerns before finalizing the settlement.

Action Items:

Practice Anchoring:

Set an initial offer or anchor in a negotiation scenario with a friend or family member and observe how it influences subsequent discussions.

Role-play Mirroring:

Pair up with a partner and practice mirroring each other's body language and communication style to build rapport and connection.

Conduct a Framing Exercise:

Select a negotiation topic and brainstorm different ways to frame the discussion to your advantage. Experiment with framing tactics and observe their impact on the negotiation dynamics.

By mastering these negotiation tactics and incorporating them into your negotiation toolkit, you'll be better equipped to navigate challenging situations and achieve successful outcomes in various personal and professional contexts.

Action Items

Practice Makes Perfect: Set up mock negotiation scenarios with friends or family members to practice your negotiation skills.

Keep a Negotiation Journal: Write down your negotiation experiences, including what worked well and what you could improve on for next time.

Reflect and Learn: After each negotiation, take some time to reflect on what went well and what you could do differently in the future.

Seek Opportunities: Look for opportunities to negotiate in your everyday life, such as deciding what game to play with friends or how to divide chores at home.

Share Your Knowledge: Teach your friends or siblings about negotiation tactics and practice together to sharpen your skills even further.

By following these action items and continuing to practice your negotiation skills, you'll become a confident and effective negotiator in no time!

Conclusion

Congratulations! You've completed Chapter 15: Mastering Negotiation. By mastering the art of negotiation and practicing the skills and tactics outlined in this chapter, you've equipped yourself with a valuable tool for achieving your goals and building stronger relationships. Remember to approach negotiations with preparation, empathy, and a willingness to collaborate for mutual benefit. With practice and perseverance, you'll become a confident and effective negotiator in no time!

Conclusion

In this journey through the Teen Wealth Code, we've explored essential principles and strategies to unlock wisdom and prosperity in the lives of teens. From understanding the elements of success to mastering negotiation tactics and embracing a millionaire mindset, each chapter has provided valuable insights and actionable steps to help you navigate the complexities of personal finance and self-development.

Recap of the Teen Wealth Code:

We began by cracking the Teen Wealth Code, delving into the importance of wisdom and prosperity and setting the stage for financial and personal growth. Through chapters dedicated to wisdom foundations, prosperity principles, and building a wealthy mindset, we've laid a strong foundation for your journey toward financial independence and personal fulfillment.

Empowering Teens to Unlock Wisdom and Prosperity:

As we conclude this journey, remember that you hold the key to your success. By embracing the principles outlined in this book and taking proactive steps to apply them in your life, you have the power to shape your future and create the life you desire. Whether it's setting big goals, mastering negotiation tactics, or cultivating a millionaire mindset, each concept is a building block on the path to unlocking your full potential.

Call to Action:

Now, I invite you to take the next step in your journey toward wisdom and prosperity. Share your thoughts and experiences with others by leaving a review of this book. Your feedback can inspire and empower fellow teens on their paths to success. Together, we can create a community of empowered individuals committed to unlocking their full potential and achieving their dreams.

Thank you for joining me on this journey through the Teen Wealth Code. Remember, the power to create the life you desire lies within you. Keep striving, keep growing, and keep unlocking new levels of wisdom and prosperity in your life.

Best wishes on your journey ahead!

Afterword

The principles in this book work. I've used them ever since I started my first job. I've taught these principles in the classroom and to adults for over 20 years. With the right mindset, success is within your grasp. Seize the opportunity!

About the Author

The principles in this book work. I've used them ever since I started my first job. I've taught these principles in the classroom and to adults for over 20 years. In addition, the author teaches communication and leadership skills to students as young as 10 through high school as well as all ages of adults.

The author graduated with a Bachelor of Science degree in Electrical Engineering from the University of Illinois, Magna Cum Laude. He obtained a Master of Management from Northwestern University – Evanston, IL with Dual Majors in Finance and Management Policy, Dean's List.